LETTERS TO MY LOVE

LETTERS TO MY LOVE

MIKLÓS RADNÓTI

Holocaust Poetry for Our Time,
translated from the Hungarian
& edited by Thomas Ország-Land

P

PENNILESS PRESS PUBLICATIONS
www.pennilesspress.co.uk

Published by Penniless Press Publications 2019

ISBN 978-1-913144-06-7

These translations are dedicated to the memory of
Irén & Jenő Ország

CONTENTS

AKNOWLEDGEMENTS

Thanks are due to the editors of the following publications and academics at the following institutions for their encouragement and advice, and for editing, publishing, teaching or exhibiting early versions of some of these poems: *Acumen, Ambit, The Jerusalem Report, Maecenas Press, New English Review, Pennine Platform, the Penniless Press, Snakeskin, Stand* (Leeds University) and *The Tern Press* as well as the Universities of Dallas, East Anglia, Edinburgh, Elte/Budapest and San Francisco.

ABOUT MIKLÓS RADNÓTI

THE AUTHOR of this book (1907–1944) was perhaps the greatest poet of the Holocaust, a Jewish Catholic convert who fell victim to a mass murder of Jews perpetrated by the regular Hungarian Army under standard orders. The crime took place towards the end of the Second World War when the Allied victory was already obvious.

Some of the poems were recovered from the grave. Today, the poems are treasured as some of the most flawless modern additions to their country's rich poetic heritage. They have gone some way towards teaching tolerance to new generations in the treatment of their racial, religious and ethnic minorities.

Other brilliant literary witnesses of the Holocaust whose work has survived, such as Anne Frank, Éva Láng and András Mezei, were children at the time. Primo Levi and Paul Celan were very young adults eventually compelled to turn to literature in order to digest and shout out their astounded pain and rage at their incomprehensible humiliation and abuse, for which they had been totally unprepared.

Unlike many others, Radnóti had plenty of opportunities to escape forced labour and death at the hands of the Nazis. He was at the height of his literary powers when he chose to enter the storm, eyes open and notebook in hand, deliberately seeking to transform the horror into poetry.

The poems recording the chaos and brutality of the Holocaust in magnificent classical metre was intended for our time, as he put it, `for reminders to future ages`. They transcend the boundaries of time and race and tribe in a universal appeal to humanity.

Read in chronological order, the poems follow the author along the highways, `down the soul's appalling deep chasms` to his death – which he describes. These intensely autobiographical pieces are about a writer stripped of all the security and comfort of civilized existence and caught up in history's insane march towards collective destruction, who yet maintains his stubborn personal dignity and concern for the future.

Radnóti went on publicly fighting back until the end, according to the legend that has grown up around his figure – which I have checked against reality in interviews with survivors of the same slave-labour camps and the eventual `deathmarch`.

The poet bribed his Hungarian guards to smuggle his work to the outside world. The notebook containing his final and most moving poems and found in the end on his body had been going around from hand to hand, enhancing the confidence of fellow prisoners in circumstances intended to undermine their faith in their own humanity.

A facsimile edition of the notebook, containing the work in careful, even handwriting and complete with printers' instructions – but in a very little known language -- was published in Hungary in 1971. Popular demand necessitated an immediate second printing. Copies of even those again became collectors' items.

Radnóti was born in Budapest and educated at Szeged University. He was prevented from pursuing an academic career because of his racial origin. He was obliged to make a meagre living mostly by literary translation. Some of his own poems were seized. Others attracted little attention. Most of Radónti's contemporaries had never heard of the poet.

He was often very wrong. He dedicated his life to becoming a `national` poet like a Petofi or Ady; he is widely remembered either as a `good` Catholic Hungarian or as a `filthy` Jew.

He introduced himself in his tragic notebook as `a Hungarian poet` despite his deprivation of Hungarian status and identity as well as civil rights.

He was murdered exactly as he had depicted the event in his very last poem. He was shot wearing a white armband identifying him as a Christian convert. There is nothing in his poetry to suggest that his clearly anticipated fate had shaken his convictions.

But a retrospective view of the Holocaust has given the survivors food for thought. Some have recovered and defended the land of Israel. Some have re-built Budapest as a vibrant Jewish cultural capital. Some have sought safety by burying their racial/cultural identity even deeper.

A foulmouthed, young, racist Hungarian politician has recently learned that he is a Jew – a fact hitherto kept from him by his protective family of Holocaust survivors. He was of course booted out from his party. He went to share his astonishment and grief with a leading Hungarian Hasidic rabbi of the same age.

And the rebbe and the rabble-rouser had lots in common. For the rabbi too had discovered his own, similarly concealed Jewish identity only at the age of 12...

I have worked on these translations most of my adult life. To me, they are a flame of hope against murderous racist bigotry, despite a current global resurgence of antisemitism.

`The great poet Radnóti knew that he would be murdered,` writes Prof. Zsuzsanna Ozsváth, a distinguished Holocaust scholar and brilliant literary translator (see `When Great Poetry Can Change the World,` Northern Review of Books, 2014).

`But he could not admit that this would happen because of his racial origin; rather, he insisted, it would occur because he was a decent human being, as he put it, One whose own blood shall at last be spilled / . . . for I have never killed. But Radnóti was not killed because of his aesthetic and moral commitment. He was killed because he was a Jew.`

Yet the insane ideology that triggered the Holocaust has blighted the lives of generations of the descendants of its authors and their followers with shame and remorse. They are now the first to cry: `Never Again!`

Radnóti could only guess whether his best and last poetry would ever be read by anyone. We know that the work has at last reached its destination and found a home in the living current of world literature.

Thomas Ország-Land,
Jerusalem, London & Budapest, 1970- 2018

JOSHU & MIRIAM

1

I am twenty-two years old. Thus
Christ too might have appeared in the autumn
at the same age when he
still had no beard, he was blond and maidens
dreamt of him nightly!

2

Just look at her hands! like dying
flowers in frost. Her hair cascading.
She's resting, a graceful dove
on a pillow. She's Mary!
but you have known and loved
girls with such faces!

*The poems above, published while their author was still a student, were
condemned by the courts for blasphemy and the poet barely escaped
exclusion from all his country`s universities.*

1930

THE BULL

Hitherto, I lived the throbbing life of a youthful bull
bored in the noonday heat among pregnant cows in the field,
running around in unending circles declaring his powers
and waving amid his game a foaming flag of saliva.
He shakes his head and turns with the splitting, thick air on his horns
and behind his stamping hooves the tormented grass and earth
spatters widely about the terrified green pasture.

And still I live like a bull, but a bull that suddenly stops
in the heart of the meadow singing with crickets, stops nostrils lifted
and sniffing the air. For he senses that far in the mountain forests
the roebuck too stops and listens and lightly flees with the wind,
the hissing wind that carries the stench of a distant wolf pack –
thus the bull snorts, but he will not escape like the deer
and considers that when his time is to come, he will fight and fall
and his bones will be scattered about in the district by the horde –
and slowly and sadly the bull bellows through the fat air.

Thus I will struggle and thus I will fall when the hour is come,
and the district will treasure my bones for reminders to future ages.

1933

BEFORE THE STORM

You sit upon the peak and on your knees asleep
that youthful woman ripened for your love; behind,
the bristly deeds of war; beware! hold dear and keep

your life, hold dear your world that you with hardened hands
have built around your life while all about you death
in circles hovered around and around above the lands –

behold, it has returned! the garden's nests from the high
treetops come plunging down in terror stricken flight,
all things are about to break! and keep an eye on the sky

because already lightning shakes the firmament;
wind tussles, drags the cradles as the men-folk whimper
asleep as weakly as the helpless innocent;

the wind blows on their dreams, they grumble and turn around,
they wake with a start and stare at you who's been awake
and sitting up amid the fleeting thunder, the sound

of roaring future battles being prepared; above,
the splendid wind speaks of the storm and so do the clouds;
it's time to wrap your woman warmly in your love.

1934

AFTERNOON, OCTOBER

Beside me, Fanni asleep beneath the oak-tree.
She had entrusted me with her last caress
to guard her peace. But so many acorns are leaping
and dropping, I feel I must quarrel with every leaf.

The autumn sunshine brightly winks through the leaves.
But fiercely humming, the menacing wasps are circling,
provoking the bickering leaves to chase the acorns
and acorn too chases acorn, unable to wait.

Now Fanni awakens. The blue in her eyes speaks of dreams.
Her delicate hands might have been drawn for an icon.
She tries to make peace between me and the foliage
and strokes my lips and touches my front teeth,

to keep me quiet. A silence ensues. It will
give way to the dribble and hiss of the raindrops, six days
of rainfall to soak the acorns away and to fasten
upon us the month of November, like a black ribbon.

1934

WAR DIARY

I. Monday Evening

These days the distant news dissolves the world
and often brings your heart to miss a beat – but
the trees of old still hold your childhood secrets
in their widening memory rings.

Between suspicious mornings and furious nights,
you have spent half your life corralled by war.
Upon the glinting points of the bayonets, striding
repression encircles you.

The land of your poetry may appear in your dreams
with the wings of freedom gliding above the meadows,
still sensed through the mist, and when the magic breaks
the elation may persist.

But you half-sit on your chair when you rarely dare
to work... restrained in grey and fearful mire.
Your hand still dignified by the pen moves forward,
more burdened day by day.

View the tide of clouds: the ravenous thunderhead
of the war is devouring the gentle blue of the sky.
With her loving, protective arms around you
sobs your anxious bride.

II. *Tuesday Evening*

I can sleep calmly now, and methodically
I go about my business... despite the gas,
grenades and bombs and aircraft made to kill me.
I'm past the fear, the rage. I cannot cry.
So I have come to live as hard as teams
of road-builders high among the windy hills:
when their light shelters
decay with age,
they build new shelters
and soundly sleep in beds of fragrant wood-shavings
and splash and dip their faces at dawn in cool
and radiant streams.

* * *

I spy out from this hilltop where I live:
the clouds are crowding.
As the watch on the mainmast over stormy seas
will bellow when, by a lightning's flash, at last
he thinks he sees
a distant land,
I also can discern from here the shores of peace:
I shout: *Compassion!*
...My voice is light.

The chilly stars respond with a brightening light,
my word is carried far by the chilly breeze
of the deepening night.

III. Weary Afternoon

A slowly dying wasp flies through the window.
My woman dreaming... muttering in her sleep.
The clouds are turning brown. Along their edges
caressed by the breeze, white ripples teem.

What can I say?... The winter comes and war comes.
I shall fall broken, abandoned without any reason
and worm-ridden earth will fill my mouth and eye-pits
and through my corpse, fresh roots will sprout.

*   *   *

Oh, peaceful, swaying afternoon, lend me your calm!
I too must rest for a while, I will work later.
Your sunrays hang suspended from the shrubs
as the evening saunters across the hill.

The blood of a fine fat cloud has smeared the sky.
And beneath the burning leaves, the scented yellow
berries are ripening, swelling with wine.

IV. *Evening Approaches*

The sun`s descending down a slippery sky.
The evening is approaching early, sprawling
along the road. The watchful moon has missed it.
Pools of mist are falling.

The evening's whirling sounds among the branches
grow louder. The hedges wake to turn and tilt
at weary travelers. These lines clasp one another
as they are slowly built.

And now!.. a squirrel invades my quiet room
and runs two brown iambic lines, a race
of terror between my window and the wall
and flees without a trace.

My fleeting peace has vanished with the squirrel.
Outside in the fields, the vermin silently spread,
digesting slowly the endless, regimented,
reclining rows of the dead.

1935-36

WALK ABOUT, CONDEMNED TO DIE

Just walk about, condemned to die!
A cat screams from the gale-torn shrubs,
a tumbling avenue of trees
confronts you and the roadway arches
its back in fear: its dust turns pale.

Just shrivel up, you autumn leaves!
and shrivel up, you dreadful world!
The cold falls hissing from the sky,
the passing wild geese drop their shadows
across the stiffened, rusty grass.

Oh poet, now you must be pure
like those who dwell on vast and windswept
snow-covered peaks, and innocent,
and innocent… like the Babe
in pious paintings of the past.

You must endure, like bleeding, wounded
wolves that trek through hostile grounds.

1936

YESTERDAY & TODAY

Yesterday two sizzling lovers with peach-ripe lips
               emerged from the kneeling shrubs in the cooling
               drizzle and, leaning each to each,
            walked past, proceeding across the meadow;

and today, ferocious cannon with muddy wheels
               emerged at daybreak with steaming soldiers –
               grey combat helmets protecting their skulls,
                 strong, heavy odours dragged by their bodies:
               the flags their of urgent, male loneliness.

(Oh, seedling blond childhood, how far you have passed!
oh, dove-white old age, I shall never reach you!
the poet stands knee-deep in slippery blood
and each song he sings is always his last.)

1936

THE FIRST ECLOGUE

Virgil, Georgics: *Quippe ubi fas versum atque nefas: tot bella per orbem,*
tam multae scelerum facies...
Trans., H. Rushton Fairclough: *For here are right and wrong inverted; so*
many wars overrun the world, so many are the shapes of sin...

Shepherd:
I have not seen you for long, did the call of the thrushes bring you?

Poet:
The woods resound with their clatter, spring must be on its way!

Shepherd:
It's not spring yet, the sky only teasing, look at that puddle,
how mildly it smiles... but when it is locked up at night by the frost
it will snarl! this is April, never be taken in by the fool –
just look, over there: the little tulips are bitten by frost.
...Why are you depressed? would you like to have a rest on a rock?

Poet:
No, I'm not even sad, I have grown so used to this horrible world
that sometimes it can't even hurt me – I'm only disgusted.

Shepherd:
Likewise. I've heard that on the wild ridges of the Pyrenees,
among corpses stiffened in blood, the red-hot cannon hold forth
and the bears and the soldiers together flee that terrible place...
that flocks of old people and women and children run with their bundles
and fling themselves to the ground when murder swoops from the skies
and the dead lie in such great heaps that no-one can clear them away...

I trust you know Frederico. Tell me, did he escape?

Poet:

He did not escape. Two years ago now he was killed in Granada.

Shepherd:

Garcia Lorca is dead! he is dead and no-one has mentioned!
News of the war can travel so fast – and, just like that,
a poet can just disappear! But was he not mourned by Europe?

Poet:

Mourned? Why, no-one has noticed. At best the wind, perhaps
when it gropes through the pyre's embers, remembers the odd broken
line of a poem that may be preserved for a frustrated future.

Shepherd:

He did not escape. Indeed, where could a poet run?
Even dear Attila* has perished – he only gestured
his *No* to the rule of the world, and who mourns his destruction?...
And how do you live these days? Does your poetry win a response?

Poet:

In the roar of the guns? Among smoking ruins, abandoned hamlets?
Still, I go on with my writing and live in this war-crazed world
like that oak over there: it knows it must fall, and although it bears
a white cross that marks it out for the woodcutter's axe tomorrow,
it bears forth new leaves regardless while awaiting its fate...
But you are fortunate. This place is calm, the wolves keep their dis-
tance
and you can forget that the flock that you tend belongs to another:
it must have been months since your master last came to call.
God bless you – must go – the night will be old before I reach home.
The moth of the evening is fluttering, shedding its silver of dusk.

===
* Attila József (1905-1937), Hungarian poet.

1938

26

SHALL I THUS WONDER...?

I lived... although I made a feeble show of life,
and I assumed that I'd be buried here, in time,
as clods of earth and rocks and years piled high above,
that while the maggot-eaten flesh disintegrates
the blind and naked bones must shiver in the dark...
I understood all that – yet hoped that, in the light,
a scuttling distant future might leaf through my lines,
despite my dust still sinking deeper in the ground.
I knew. But tell me! Has the work, the work survived?

1938

THE WITNESS

I am a poet, and I'd be rejected
even if I mumbled in disgrace,
de-daa, de-daa... no matter: lots of devils
are happy to sing in my place.

I've justified, believe me, every caution,
the searching eyes and ears of every sleuth!
For I'm a poet destined for the stake,
a witness who tells the truth.

A poet – and I've noted what I've seen,
that snow is white and blood and poppies red
and that the poppies' downy stems are green.*

I know my own blood shall in time be spilled
...for I have never killed.

==================================

* Red, white & green: the Hungarian tricolour

1939

FLAMES FLUTTERING...

Small flames are fluttering and slowly and forever dying –
along the bright meridians, the souls of the soldiers flying.
Souls all alike! no matter who each one had been or done
exposed to screaming icy winds or oppressed by the searing sun,
all serving by cannon, drunk with longing, vomiting in the grip
of crippling fear... all sailors onboard a heaving battleship!
The watch is kept by sensitive death. Below, mines grimly glide.
From time to time, their slimy harvest washed up by the tide –
a swaying catch of corpses and shattered dolphins, lifeless spawn.
There too, the sun still rises, but no-one welcomes such a dawn.
High up, an aircraft rumbles. Its advance across the sky
reflected by its silent shadow drawn upon the sly,
dark waters. Whirlpools hiss towards it. Signals flash their grief...
and blooms of human blood will deepen the red of the coral reef.
The peril howls all day. Light oil seeps from the fine machine.
The ship is tracked by echoing rage, like a hostile submarine.
At last, the sun is drowned in smoke and, like a terrified,
a writhing face, the moon appears upon the other side,
and flames are fluttering again and slowly forever dying –
Along the bright meridians, the souls of the soldiers flying.

1939

OF THE WIFE: A DOTTY SONG

She's come! The door is bursting into laughter.
The thirsty flowerpots gape with secret trembles
and, in her hair, a sleepy, slim, blonde streak
chirps up… a frightened sparrow's tiny cry.

A breathless, blackened light-flex squeaks with joy
and twists its awkward shapes in space towards her.
All objects leap. They spin. I can't keep track.

She has come home, she'd been away all day.
She holds a petal from a giant poppy
and uses that to drive away my death.

1940

FOAMING SKY

The moon is rocking on a foaming sky –
I am amazed that I'm alive.
Tenacious death is searching through our time;
its breath turns people ashen.

The year looks back from time to time and screams
appalled, and looks again and faints.
What pain-dulled autumn skulks once more behind me,
and what a ruinous winter!

The woodland bled, and in the whirling time
each hour bled. And in the snow
the scrawling wind recorded dreadful numbers
upon the killing fields.*

I've lived to see a lot. The air is weighty.
A lukewarm silence masking tiny,
disturbing, distant, muffled sounds surrounds
me – like before my birth.

At last, I pause. I rest beneath a tree.
It rustles in a frightening rage.
A branch then reaches down. To throttle me?
I'm neither frail nor faint-hearted,

just tired. So I freeze. The hostile branch
frisks through my hair in nervous silence.
I should forget it… No, I've never yet
forgotten anything.

The rushing foam engulfs the climbing moon.
A streak of dark-green poison creeps
across the sky. I slowly roll a cigarette,
with care. Still, I'm alive.

---

*This poem mourns the WW2 dismemberment of Poland that was followed shortly by the "resettlement" and murder of up to 18,000 Hungarian Jews in Galicia/Ukraine.

(June 8, 1940)

LIKE A PREGNANT WOMAN

A raven, like a pregnant woman, waddles
across the road that lies in peace again.
At last a bird, thank goodness! sighs the road,
and pours out all her recent woes and pain.

The wounded crops are also listening.
The battle-broken district rests her eyes...
she still remembers, even though the evening
approaches softly with sweet lullabies.

A small live landmine lurking in the ground –
it darkly dreams of death but would not dare
to detonate... its raging urge restrained
by a cabbage with a disapproving glare.

Behind the sagely drooping sunflowers, yonder,
afloat beneath young trees above the mud
extends a horizontal steel-blue cloud:
dense razor-wire, still tense with thirst for blood.

But when the dews of dawn caress the wire,
a yellow flower creeps along a narrow
gap carefully (its tender stalk a fuse)
and opens gold – the flower of the marrow.

And silence will again spray on the land
and storks alight where parapets stand now...
The trenches are abandoned to the rabbits,
but Flórián will put them to the plough.

The men will take up their neglected crafts –
the former weavers once again will make
good clothes and nightly dream of threads until
in pearly mornings peacefully they wake.

The women will again bend to their chores
and by their feet, a clamorous world will grow
of graceful girls in poppy-coloured dresses
and boys like butting kids, so far to go...

Thus will return the wise eternal order
evolved beneath the stars within the pool
of life, the scheme of animals and crops,
a strict but tame, unmilitary rule.

(1941)

IN YOUR ARMS

In your arms I lie, you rock me
quietly.
In my arms you lie, I rock you
quietly.
In your arms I lie, an infant,
silently.
In my arms you are a child, I'm
hearkening, watching, sensing you.
In your arms, I'm locked embraced
when I'm alarmed.
In my arms, embracing you, I'm
not alarmed.
In your arms, the great, the final
stream of silence
will not frighten me.
In your arms, death will arrive –
light and graceful,
like a dream.

1941

THE SECOND ECLOGUE

Pilot:
Last night we flew so far that I had to laugh in rage;
their fighters droned like bee-swarms trying to engage
us from above with strong defensive fire – but, my friend,
our fresh squadrons showed up on the horizon in the end.
I thought they'd prang and pick me up with dust pan and brush
but I'm back, see! Tomorrow, cowardly Europe can rush
again to air-raid shelters to hide from me while it may...
but never mind, friend. Did you write since yesterday?

Poet:
I did, what else could I do? The poet writes his lines,
the pussy cat miaows and the puppy whines,
the fishy coyly spawns. I write about everything
so even you should know, up there, while soldiering,
how I live when the bloodshot sick moonlight staggers down
among the ruined streets as the bombs destroy the town,
walls cave in, homes explode, the squares curl up in fright,
breath falters, even the sky is disgusted with the sight,
the bombers come, persistent, sometimes they disappear
to swoop in rattling frenzy on the houses drowned in fear!
I write, what else could I do... Poems too can be vicious
and dangerous, you know, odd lines are too capricious
for words, demanding bravery... The poet writes his lines,
the pussy cat miaows and the puppy whines,
the fish – and so on. Can you make... anything? No! you sit
fused with your friend the engine. Admit it: your eardrums split
down here because you cannot hear the roar of the plane.
How will you feel when flying over us again?

Pilot:
You'll laugh. I fly in fear... desiring, up, above,
to lie on a bed, eyes closed, caressing with my love.
Or just to hum about her and to conjure up such a scene
daydreaming in the steamy chaos of the canteen.
When I am up, I'd come down! down here, I long to fly,
without a place of my own between my own earth and sky.

I have grown much too fond of the aeroplane too, I know,
we've learned to share a rhythm of pain so long ago...
You understand – and please... write about me! make it known
that I too was a man: destructive, homeless, alone
above and below. Who will grasp the causes of my deed?...
Explain me, won't you?

        Poet:

                If I live – with some who still want to read.

                        1941

THE THIRD ECLOGUE

My pastoral muse! Accompany me to this sleepy coffeehouse
away from your light-drenched, misty riverbank and its loosely
erected molehills, its sightless moles and your sunburnt fishermen
of noble proportions and white and healthy teeth, stretched out
asleep in their slippery barges after the morning catch!

My pastoral muse, accompany me to this urban district –
Those seven carousing travelling salesmen should not deter you:
pathetic losers, they cannot resist the pressures of business...
nor should those doctors of law to the right: not one of whom can
still master a simple flute... but look: how they suck their cigars!

Accompany me! I'm a teacher and, between classes, I've chosen
this place for a moment's peace in the smoke to muse on affection.
A tweet from a bird can revive the juices of an old poplar.
A call from a woman has flung me high to the distant peaks
of wild, adolescent desire... that bygone terrain of youth.

My pastoral muse, assist me! Today, the triumphant trumpets
of dawn resounded in praise of the love she bestows upon me,
the fleeting flash of her smile, and the joyful, dancing rhythm
of sighs that escape her lips, and the fragrance, feel and form
and heat and cool of her flesh, and the way it reflects the moon...

My pastoral muse, assist me! Allow me to ponder on passion
despite my vast and nagging sadness, despite the unending
despair that hounds me through this world. I know I shall perish.
The trees grow twisted in my dreams and mine pits collapse
and I can hear the scream of the very bricks in the walls.

My pastoral muse, assist me – for even the sky is falling!
The poets dying in droves. No mounds will guard our dust, nor
such graceful urns as back in the classical past – only random,
surviving fragments of verse. How then can I serenade life?
However... her body is calling. Assist me, my pastoral muse!

1941

ENCHANTMENT

We're sitting in the brightness
and scowling in the glare,
a rosebush is leaping
over the hedgerow,
the light leaping also
as the rain-clouds gather,
lightning streaks by
and the lash of thunder
clashes with thunder
again and again, high
high up in the sky,
below them the blue
of the lake is withering,
its waters rising –
come into the house
and take off your dress,
out there it is raining,
and take off your blouse
and let the rain, the rain
wash our hearts together.

1942

THE FOURTH ECLOGUE

The Poet:
No! – You should have asked me before I was born.
No! – I knew the answer. I knew, I knew.
No! – I screamed my retort to this brutal world:
No! – Its darkness pounds me! Its light cuts me through!
…All that howling only strengthened my lungs.
I've survived. My skull has only hardened.

The Voice:
The crimson waves of measles and scarlet-fever
both tossed you safely ashore. And once a lake was
about to swallow you – but it spat you out.
So why do you think that time has embraced you, why?
And why do your lungs' great wings, your heart, your liver,
your moist, mysterious, entity serve you, why? –
And even cancer, that deadly, fearful flower,
may not have spread its roots within your flesh.

The Poet:
I was born, protesting. I'm alive.
I've grown up. What for? I do not know.
All my life, I have desired freedom.
All my life, I've been escorted by guards.

The Voice:
You have ascended to wind-worn, radiant, peaks.
You have beheld a kneeling, humble fawn
at dusk among the shrubs of the mountain side
and watched a tree-trunk's resin drop in the sunlight
and seen a naked woman emerge from the river…
A stag-beetle once alighted on your palm.

The Poet:
Even such visions disappear in bondage.
Would I were but a bird, a word or a mountain,
just a fleeting, consoling thought or a gesture

39

momentarily, boastfully mimicking God –
Liberty, help me at last to find my home!

Give me the peaks, the wood, the shrubs, the woman!
Show me the blazing wings of the soul in the wind!
Let me be born anew to a better world
where the rising sunlight heralds a promising
day emerging through the golden vapours…

Silence prevails. But I sense the breath of a storm.
Ripening fruit are swaying from the branches.
Lightly tossed by the breeze, a drifting butterfly
balances. Death is whispering in the garden.

Now I can see: I'm too maturing for death.
Soon the waves of time that bore me high must
plunge me down. My captive isolation
slowly grows, like the crescent of the moon.

I shall find my freedom. The earth will unbind me
while, above me, this routed world is finally
burnt away. The writing tablets are shattered.
Soaring imagination, spread out your wings!

The Voice:
The fruit of the garden must sway and ripen and fall.
Your pain will end in the deep earth steeped in memories.
Till then, let the smoke of your anger rise, and learn
to write upon the skies, if all else be broken.

(1943)

A HESITANT ODE

How long I have prepared, dear, to describe to you
the secret constellation of my love,
perhaps its substance only, just in a single image.
Your teeming sense within me floods like life itself
and sometimes it is timeless, certain and secure:
eternal like a fossil shell within a rock.
The silken, feline moonlit night above my head
begins the hunt for buzzing tiny dreams in flight.
And still I have not managed to describe to you
how much it means to me to sense your caring gaze
as it hesitates upon my hand when I'm at work.
No similes will do. I scrap them as they come.
I will begin this whole attempt again tomorrow
because I am worth only as much as the words
within this poem, and my search will keep me going
until I am reduced to bones and tufts of hair.
You're tired. It's been a long day for me also.
What can I say? The objects, look! exchange their glances
in praise of you; a broken cube of sugar sings
on the table; and a drop of honey falls and, like
a ball of gold, it glitters on the tablecloth;
spontaneously now, an empty tumbler rings out:
it's glad it lives with you. Perhaps I'll have the time
to tell you what it's like when it expects you home.
Descending darkly, flocks of dreams approach you lightly,
they flit away yet keep returning to your brow.
Your drowsy eyes still send a last farewell towards me.
Your loosened hair cascades in freedom. You're asleep.
The lengthy shadow of your eyelids softly flutters.
Your hand, a resting birch twig, falls upon my pillow.
I share your peace, for you are not a different world;
and even here I sense as a multitude of secret
and thin, sage lines relax in the tranquil palm of your hand.

1943

THE FIFTH ECLOGUE
In memoriam György Bálint*

A Fragment

My dear friend, how I shuddered and shivered from the chill
of this poem, and dreaded the news about you... and fled from it!
And I could scribble but broken lines.
                                    And I tried to write
on other themes: but in vain! this frightful, secretive night
commands me: *You must speak of him.*
                                    I flinch, but the voice
goes silent again like the slain in the pastures of Ukraine.
You're missing.
                    Even this autumn has brought no news
                                                of you.
Out there, in the woods, the winter grimly whispers its prophecy
as heavy clouds migrate across the sky. They halt.
Perhaps you are alive... who knows? –
                                    I do not.
                                            And I rage
no more when people shrug and cover their faces in pain.
And no-one can tell.
                    But... are you alive? Or, might you be wounded
and walking the forest floor in the heady fragrance of mud,
or have you become but a scent?...
                                    Snowflakes light on the fields.
Just missing. This news: what a blow!
                                    My heart beats a numb re-
sponse.
Between my two ribs arises a throbbing pain at such times,
when I recall your words, heard long ago, with such sharpness,
and I sense your physical substance with such precision as though
you were dead –
                    And even today... I still cannot write about you!

1943

===
* György Báint (1906-1943) writer, translator & critic, enlisted in a
slave-labour battalion attached to the Hungarian invasion force in
Ukraine, listed missing in 1943.

HOW OTHERS SEE...

How others see this region, I cannot understand:
to me, this little country is menaced motherland
engulfed by flames, the world of my childhood swaying far,
and I am grown from this land as tender branches are
from trees. And may my body sink into this soil in the end.
When plants reach out towards me, I greet them as a friend
and know their names and flowers. I am at home here, knowing
the people on the road and I know where they are going –
and how I know the meaning when, by a summer lane,
the sunset paints the walls with a liquid flame of pain!
The pilot is trained to interpret a war map from the sky,
and even Vörösmarty's* old house escapes his eye;
what can he identify here? grim barracks and factories,
but I see steeples, oxen, and grasshoppers, farms and bees;
his lens spies out the vital production plants, the fields,
but I can see the worker, afraid below, who shields
his labour, a singing orchard, a vineyard and a wood,
among the graves a granny still mourning her widowhood;
and what may seem a plant or a rail line that must be wrecked
is just a signal-house with the keeper standing erect
and waving his red flag, lots of children around the guard;
a shepherd dog might roll in the dust in a factory yard;
and there's the park with the footprints of past loves and the flavour
of childhood kisses – the honey, the cranberry I still savour,
and on my way to school, by the kerbside, to postpone
a spot-test one certain morning, I stepped upon a stone:
look! there's the stone whose magic the pilot cannot see...
No instrument could merge them in his typography.

True, most of us are guilty, our people like the rest.
We know our faults. We know how and when we have transgressed.
But blameless lives are among us, of toil and poetry and passion,
and infants with an infinite capacity for compassion –
they will protect its glow down in gloomy bomb shelters, till
our land is marked out again by the finger of peace... then they will
respond to our muffled words with new voices fresh and bright.

Extend your vast wings above us, protective cloud of night.

==

* Mihály Vörösmarty (1800-1855), poet.
                    January 17, 1944

OLD PRISONS

The stillness of old prisons, true, sublime
  old fashioned suffering and noble death,
poetic death... heroic, lofty view,
  composed and measured talk and due attention –
How far you are! Oblivion receives
  one who still dares to move. The fog descends.
Reality has lost its form and content,
  and, like a shattered pot, its strews about
its shards: untrue, incoherent perceptions.

What will become of you who would discuss,
while still allowed to live, reality
in formal terms, and teach the art of judgment?

I would still teach, though all has burst asunder.
I sit. I stare. No more is left to do.

March 27, 1944

UPON A JABBERING PALM

Upon a jabbering palm-tree
crouching, I should be rather,
a free soul in earthly matter,
shivering, down from heaven

where sage scholastic apes
would keep me company,
their calls, like a sharp and shiny
shower, wash over me

and I would chant with the team
in merry cacophony,
and cheer the harmonious hue
of their rumps and noses whose shades
of blue would seem the same...

and above the enchanted tree
a giant sun would pace,
and there I would bemoan
my shame for the human race

and the apes would grasp my pain,
for still, the apes are sane –
and Oh! in their company
if I might share their merciful
good death beneath that tree...

(April 5, 1944)

NEITHER MEMORIES NOR MAGIC

Concealed, my many angers lay in my heart before
this hour as brown seeds ripen within the apple-core,
and I was always certain that, sword in hand, a friendly
strong angel followed behind me, an angel to defend me.
But when, one wild dawn, waking, you see your whole world crum-
bling
to dust and must go forward confused, a phantom fumbling
and all but naked, your few belongings left behind,
then you will find arising in your lightened heart, a refined
and musing, humble yearning, laconic and mature –
if still you can rebel, it's not over your own sorrow
but for a glowing, distant, sweet freedom for tomorrow.

Positions and possessions I've never held and won't,
but spare a moment's thought for this wealthy life: I don't
concern myself with vengeance, my heart is free of rage,
the world will be rebuilt – and, although this ugly age
has banned my words, they will yet ring out beneath new walls;
alone I must live through all that in my time befalls
me knowing that neither memories nor magic can defend me;
I will not glance behind me – above, the sky's unfriendly,
and should you see me yet, turn away, my friend, and go on.
Where in the past a mighty protector stood behind me,
the angel… might be gone.

April 30, 1944

THE HUNTED

From my window I see a hillside,
   it cannot see me at all;
I'm still, verse trickles from my pen
   but nothing matters in hiding;
I see, though cannot grasp this solemn,
   old-fashioned grace: as ever,
the moon emerges onto the sky and
   the cherry tree bursts into blossom.

May 9, 1944

FRAGMENT

I lived upon this earth in such an age
when folk were so debased they sought to murder
for pleasure, not just to comply with orders.
Their faith in falsehoods drove them to corruption.
Their lives were ruled by raving self-deceptions.

I lived upon this earth in such an age
that idolized the sly police informers,
whose heroes were the killers, spies and thieves –
The few who merely held their peace or failed
to cheer were loathed like victims of the plague.

I lived upon this earth in such an age
when those who risked protest were wise to hide
and gnaw their fists in self-consuming shame –
The country grinned towards its dreadful fate
insane and wild and drunk on blood and mire.

I lived upon this earth in such an age...
The mother of an infant was a curse
and pregnant women were glad to abort.
The living envied the corpses in the graves
while on the table foamed their poisoned cup.
....
....

I lived upon this earth in such an age...
when even the poet fell silent awaiting, expecting
an ancient, terrible voice to resound – for one
alone could utter a fitting curse on such horror,
that scholar of weighty words: the prophet Isaiah.

May 19, 1944

49

THE SEVENTH ECLOGUE

Evening approaches the barracks, and the ferocious oak fence
braided with barbed wire, look, dissolves in the twilight.
Slowly the eye thus abandons the bounds of our captivity
and only the mind, the mind is aware of the wire's tension.
Even fantasy finds no other path towards freedom.
Look, my beloved, dream, that lovely liberator,
releases our aching bodies. The captives set out for home.

Clad in rags and snoring, with shaven heads, the prisoners
fly from Serbia's blinded peaks to their fugitive homelands.
Fugitive homeland! Oh – is there still such a place?
still unharmed by bombs? as on the day we enlisted?
And will the groaning men to my right and my left return safely?
And is there a home where hexameters are appreciated?

Dimly groping line after line without punctuation,
here I write this poem as I live in the twilight, inching
like a bleary-eyed caterpillar, my way on the paper –
everything, torches and books, all has been seized by the *Lager*
guard, our mail has stopped and the barracks are muffled by fog.

Riddled with insects and rumours, Frenchmen, Poles, loud Italians,
separatist Serbs and dreamy Jews live here in the mountains –
fevered, a dismembered body, we lead a single existence,
waiting for news, a sweet word from a woman, and decency, freedom,
guessing the end still obscured by the darkness, dreaming of miracles.

Lying on boards, I am a captive beast among vermin,
the fleas renew their siege but the flies have at last retired.
Evening has come; my captivity, behold, is curtailed
by a day and so is my life. The camp is asleep. The moonshine
lights up the land and highlights the taut barbed wire fence,
it draws the shadow of armed prison guards, seen through the window,
walking, projected on walls, as they spy the night's early noises.

Swish go the dreams, behold my beloved, the camp is asleep,
the odd man who wakes with a snort turns about in his little space
and resumes his sleep at once, with a glowing face. Alone
I sit up awake with the lingering taste of a cigarette butt
in my mouth instead of your kiss, and I get no merciful sleep,
for neither can I live nor die without you, my love, any longer.

Lager Heidenau, above Zagubica,
in the mountains,

July, 1944

LETTER TO MY WIFE

Mute worlds lie in the depths, their stillness crying
inside my head; I shout: no-one's replying
in war-dazed, silenced Serbia the distant,
and you are far away. My dreams, persistent,
are woven nightly in your voice, and during
the day it's in my heart still reassuring –
and thus I keep my silence while, profoundly
detached, the cooling bracken stirs around me.

No longer can I guess when I will see you,
who were once firm and sure as psalms can be – you,
as lovely as the shadow and the light – you,
whom I could seek out mute, deprived of sight – you,
now with this landscape you don't know entwined – you,
projected to the eyes, but from the mind – you,
once real till to the realm of dreams you fell – you,
observed from my own puberty's deep well – you,

nagged jealously in my soul for a truthful
pledge that you love me, that upon the youthful
proud peak of life you'll be my bride; I'm yearning
and then, with sober consciousness returning,
I do remember that you are my wife and
my friend – past three wild frontiers, terrified land.
Will autumn leave me here forgotten, aching?
My memory's sharper over our lovemaking;

I once believed in miracles, forgetting
their age; above me, bomber squadrons setting
against the sky where I just watched the spark and
the colour of your eyes – the blue then darkened,
the bombs then longed to fall. I live despite them
and I am captive. I have weighed up, item
by painful item, all my hopes still tended –
and will yet find you. For you, I've descended,

along the highways, down the soul's appalling
deep chasms. I shall transmit myself through falling
live flames or crimson coals to conquer the distance,
if need be learn the treebark's tough resistance –
the calm and might of fighting men whose power
in danger springs from cool appraisal shower
upon me, bringing sober strength anew,
and I become as calm as 2 x 2.

Lager Heidenau,
August-September,

1944

À LA RECHERCHE...

Gentle past evenings, you too are ennobled through recollection!
Brilliant table adorned by poets and their young women,
where have you slid in the mud of the memory? where is the night
when the exuberant friends still merrily drank the native
wine of the land from slender glasses that sparkled their glances?

Lines of poetry swam around the glow of the lamps
and bright green adjectives swayed on the foaming crest of the metre
and still the dead were alive, the prisoners home, and the dear
vanished friends wrote verse, those fallen long ago whose hearts
lie under the soil of Spain and Flanders and Ukraine.

Some of them charged forward gritting their teeth in the fire and fought
only because there was nothing they could do to avoid it,
and while their company fitfully slept around them under
the soiled shelter of night, they remembered their rooms of the past,
calm caves and islands, their retreat from this society.

Some of them travelled helpless in sealed cattle trucks to places,
some stood numbly waiting unarmed in frozen minefields,
some also went voluntarily, silent with guns in their hands
for clearly they saw their personal place and role in the fighting –
now the angel of freedom guards their great dreams in the night.

Some... doesn't matter. Where have the wise, winy evenings vanished?
Swift swarmed the draft-notes and swift multiplied the poetic fragments
as did the wrinkles around the lips and eyes of the wives
with enchanting smiles. The elf-footed girls grew dull
and heavy in loneliness over the silent and endless war years.

Where is the night, the tavern and, under the lime trees, that table?
Where are the living and where are the others trampled in battle?
Still, my heart hears their voices, my hand still holds their handshakes,
thus I quote their works and behold their proportions and stature,
silent prisoner myself in Serbia's wailing mountains.

54

Where is the night? Such a night perhaps may never recur, for death
gives always a different perspective to all that has vanished.
They still sit at the table, they hide in the smiles of the women,
and they will sip from our glasses, the friends still unburied and wait-
ing,
lying in distant forests, asleep in foreign pastures.

Lager Heidenau,
August 17, 1944

THE EIGHTH ECLOGUE

Poet:

Greetings, handsome old man, how swiftly you climb this rugged
mountain path! Are you lifted by wings or pursued by an army?
Wings lift you, passion drives you, lightning burns in your eyes –
greetings, grand old traveller, I comprehend that you must be
one of the ancient wrathful prophets – but, tell me, which one?

Prophet:

Which one? Nahum am I, from the city of Elkosh, who cursed
the lewd Assyrian city of Nineveh, chanted the holy
word with a vengeance. I was a vessel brimming with rage!

Poet:

I know your ancient rage as your writing has survived.

Prophet:

It has survived. But evil multiplies faster today,
and the Lord's purpose is still unknown to this very day;
for clearly the Lord has said the majestic rivers would dry up,
Carmel would weaken, the flower of Bashan and Lebanon wither,
and mountains would tremble and finally fire consume it all.
It all came to pass.

Poet:

             The nations rush to slaughter each other;
like once Nineveh, now humanity's soul is degraded.
Did proclamations and ravenous, hellish, green clouds of locusts
serve any purpose? man must be surely the basest of creatures!
Tiny babes smashed to death against brick-walls in many places,
church towers turned into flaming torches, houses turned
into ovens, their residents roasting. Factories go up in smoke.
Screaming, the streets run with people on fire and stumble and faint.
Stirring, the heavy door of the bomb-bay opens above, leaving
corpses on city squares lying shrunken as cow-pats on meadows.
All you have prophesied is fulfilled again. So tell me,
what made you leave the primeval vortex again to return
to earth?

Prophet:
My anger. That humans should remain so utterly lonely
all this time while surrounded by armies of human-shaped heathens –
Also, I'd like to behold again the fall of the sinful
cities, to see and to tell, to bear witness to future ages.

Poet:
But you have spoken already. The Lord has said through your words:
Woe to the fortifications laden with loot, to the bastions
built of corpses! Tell me, in all the millennia, what
has fanned your anger to rage with such obstinate, heavenly burning?

Prophet:
Back in ancient times, the Lord touched my mis-shaped lips
with His burning coals (as He also touched wise Isaiah's), thus He
searched my heart; the embers were hot and glowing, an angel
held them with tongs. "Behold," I cried to the Lord, "I am waiting,
ready to go out to spread Your word." Once sent out
by the Lord, one neither has age nor peace ever after;
the fire of heaven burns in one's lips through the ages. And how long
is for the Lord a millennium? Only a fleeting instant.

Poet:
You're very young, I envy you, father! How could I presume
to measure my life by your awesome age? Already, my time
wears me down – like rushing rivers wear down the pebbles.

Prophet:
Only you think so. I know your latest poetry. Anger
keeps you alive. The rage of prophets and poets is similar,
food and drink to the people! It will sustain those who want
to survive till the birth of the kingdom promised by that disciple,
by that that young rabbi who came to fulfil the law and our words.
Come with me to announce that the hour is already near,
that country about to be born. What might be, then, the Lord's purpose?
Now you can see that it is that country. Let us set forth
and gather the people, bring your wife and cut two staffs,
for staffs make good companions for wanderers. Look, I'd like that
one,

I like a firm, knotty hold on a staff... gnarled and strong and uneven.

Lager Heidenau,

August 23, 1944

DEATHMARCH

Collapsed exhausted, only a fool would rise again
to drag his knees and ankles once more like marching pain
yet press on as though wings were to lift him on his way,
invited by the ditch but in vain, he'd dare not stay...
Ask him, why not? maintaining his pace, he might reply:
he longs to meet the wife and a kinder death. That's why.
But he's insane, that poor man, because above the homes,
since we have left them, only a scorching whirlwind roams.
The walls are laid. The plum tree is broken. And the night
lurks bristling as a frightened, abandoned mongrel might.
Oh, if I could believe that all things for which I yearn
exist beyond my heart, that there's still home and return...
return! the old veranda, the peaceful hum of bees
attracted by the cooling fresh plum jam in the breeze,
the still, late summer sunshine, the garden drowsing mute,
among the leaves the swaying voluptuous naked fruit,
and Fanni waiting for me, blonde by the russet hedge,
while languidly the morning re-draws the shadow's edge...
It may come true again – see, the moon, so round! – be wise...
Don't leave me, friend, shout at me! shout... and I will arise!

Bor,
September 15, 1944

PICTURE POSTCARDS

I

The roar of cannon rolls from Bulgaria dense and broad,
resounds upon the mountain crest, hesitates and ceases;
the maned sky runs above; but recoils the neighing road;
and men and beasts are tangled, and wagon, thought and load.
You're deep and constant in me despite this turbulence
and glowing in my conscience, forever still, intense
and silent like an angel when wondering he sees
destruction, or like beetles entombed in dying trees.

In the mountains,
August 30, 1944

II

Nine kilometers from here, look! the haystacks
and homes consumed in blaze,
the peasants smoke in silence by the meadow
and huddle in a daze.
But here, the shepherdess leaves in the water
light ripples in her wake
and gently dipping down, her curly flock drinks
the clouds up in the lake.

Cservenka,
October 6, 1944

III

The oxen slaver red saliva. People
pass urine mixed with blood. My squadron stands
disorganized in filthy bunches. Death
blows overhead its cold, infernal breath.

Mohács,
October 24, 1944

IV

I tumble near his body. It turns over
already taut like string about to break.
Shot through the nape. *You too will end up like that,*
I mutter to myself. *Lie calm. Be patient.*
The flower of death unfolds in fear. I wait.
Blood mixed with dirt grows clotted on my ear.
I hear a soldier quip: *He'll get away yet.*

Szentkirályszabadja,
October 31, 1944

AN EPILOGUE,
by the Translator

Unmarked the moment when our forebears lost
our innocence to automated killing.
The prisoners' feet were kissed by winter frost.
Their hunger ached. Some gave up hope, unwilling
to stumble on with pride and will run out.

They deemed a small delay a meagre prize,
fell gently and remained there calm and solemn,
unless one were to shout at them to rise,
awaiting death behind the marching column –
Some people had the stubborn strength to shout.

They've left to us the throb of phantoms' feet
and principles esteemed by every nation,
a world of wealthy customers to eat
the feast of plenty set by automation –
and now and then a fearful, halting doubt:

when warplanes scrape across the sky a scar
above our loved ones' heads or when the telly
brings for our entertainment from afar
a child with hunger bloated in the belly –
and we have lost the voice or will to shout.

Further Reading:
1
How the Murderer of a Poet Has Become a Hero in Hungary (2010)

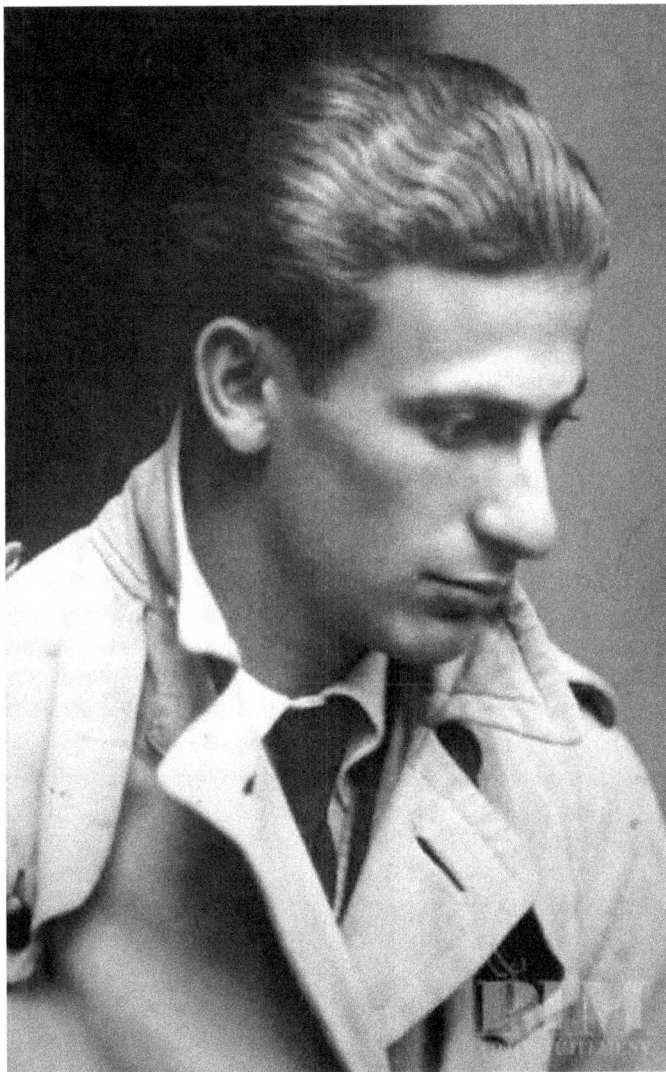

Miklós Radnóti (1909-1944)

THE COMMANDER of the death-squad personally responsible for the murder of Miklós Radnóti escaped retribution for the deed. His remains rest in official burial grounds reserved for the heroes of the Hungarian republic.

This has been established by Tamás Csapody, a noted jurist and sociologist. His revelations, published prominently by the country's leading literary and political journals, are of particular interest in the context of widening current antisemitism sweeping Eastern Europe.

Radnóti was shot at the age of 35 in 1944, a victim of the National Socialists' attempt at the "ethnic cleansing" of Europe. He was condemned with a group Jewish-Hungarian prisoners because of their inability to keep up with a Westward "deathmarch". Their bodies were dumped in a mass grave.

The circumstances of the massacre are even worse than the many myths current about the event. It was carried out by the Royal Hungarian Army, not some "foreign" ethnic Germans hitherto blamed by the literary establishment. And two members of the five-man death squad positively identified in secret inquiries after the war were allowed to go free. The reason: they had by then joined the ruling Communist Party.

Until now, his murder has been shrouded by misinformation. In common with the opinion shapers of the rest of formerly Soviet-dominated Europe, most of Hungary's teachers and editors have not even begun to digest the shameful role their country played during the war.

Holocaust poetry is therefore an irritant here. Generations of Hungarian school children have been required to recite Randnóti by heart, but they have been taught that the poems were about the general horrors of war rather than specific genocide. They have been told that the poet had met a "tragic death"—but not that it was racist murder committed with the approval or connivance of the majority of Hungarians at the time.

Yet the spirit of his poetry has miraculously survived and won the affection of the nation. Radnóti today is perhaps the best loved by the Hungarian public among all its poets of the recent past. His name fills auditoriums. His lines are quoted at public meetings. Hence the prolonged furor over the revelations of the circumstances of his murder.

Unknown to the public, the facts were reliably established shortly after the war by confidential inquiries conducted under the authority of the interior ministry. This was done in order to forestall any hitch to the smooth administration of the Communist order. The archives of the ministry at last exposed to researchers are belatedly rewriting history.

Their contents form the core of Csapody's evidence, corroborated by the records of slave labour camps in Serbia where Radnóti and some 6,000 other Hungarian Jews were deployed in the war, about half of whom perished. Csapody matched his findings with testimonials by survivors and material in the archives of Jad Vasem, Belgrade, Berlin and Budapest.

Csapody is a widely published, highly respected intellectual and author of *Civil Scenarios*, a collection of essays on principal aspects of the Hungarian transition process. He has published several specialist papers during recent years on his researchers into Radnóti's murder and the Serbian slave camps near Bor.

But the issue has burst into the public domain only through the recent publication of major articles by him in the authoritative *Népszabadság* newspaper and the literary journal *Élet és Irodalom*. These articles have been reprinted by many other newspapers, and the subject taken up by many other writers.

Csapody writes that the Bor camps were supervised by the Germans but administered by the Hungarians with senseless sadism. They were vacated late in 1944 as part of the German retreat, its inmates despatched westwards in an infamous "deathmarch".

Their weakened captives were driven at a forced pace under the blows of their armed escorts who were themselves being harassed by the Serbian partisans. People were being murdered at no provocation.

In a rare gesture of humanity, Radnóti and 21 others who could not keep the pace were put on horse-drawn wagons under the command of Sergeant András Tálas. He was ordered to take them to hospital. But they were not accepted.

He might have decided to abandon them in the prevailing chaos with impunity. He chose to murder them instead. Witness testimonials made by Tálas' subordinates state that he drew his handgun and led the massacre.

Tálas was recognized after the war by a former Bor inmate. He was tried and executed in 1947 for other war crimes. His body was buried in parcel No. 298 at Rákoskeresztúr cemetery in Budapest, together with those of other war criminals.

But after the eventual collapse of Soviet administration here, a simplistic public honours committee mistakenly assumed that all people executed by the Communists had sacrificed their lives for freedom. Or was this a deliberate act of neo-Nazi mischief? (The chairman of the committee then was and still is Péter Boross, a former Hungarian prime minister.) The funeral grounds of shame thus became a resting-place reserved for the "martyrs" of the nation.

Today, Tálas' grave is furnished with all the trappings of honour that the living can lavish on the dead. His name has been at last removed from the list of "heroes" borne by a commemorative plaque, but those of other presumed war criminals are still present.

No one suggests that the confusion has been cleared up by the removal of Tálas' name. The grounds regularly receive ceremonial visits by state dignitaries and school children. Csapody and other lovers of Radnóti's poetry argue that at least this should cease until another, better advised honours committee thinks its way out of the memorial mess.

According to incomplete and often unreliable records, the remains resting in parcel No. 298 include those of at total of 51 people condemned for war crimes. Their status is confusing because the notoriously unprofessional, Communist-controlled, post-war tribunals that condemned them often handed down hasty and harsh sentences driven by political rather than judicial considerations in the tradition of the Moscow show trials.

The issue thus reflects the confusion of values in Hungary's current, painful transition from a humiliated subject state towards a functioning democracy. The controversy is a matter of great practical significance because the declared choice of a country's public heroes may influence the behaviour of its future leaders.

2
Books:
For more information about the experience of Hungarian Jews during and around WW2, see the following:

Neil Astley (ed.) *The Hundred Years' War: Modern War Poems*, Bloodaxe Books, UK, 2014

John Bierman, *Righteous Gentile*, Penguin Books, London, 1981

George Eisen, *Children and Play in the Holocaust: Games among the Shadows*, Massachusetts University Press, 1988 and Corvina Press, Budapest 1990

Kinga Frojimovics *et. al*, *Jewish Budapest: Monuments, Rites, History*, Central European University Press, Budapest, 1999

Agnes Gergely, *Requiem for a Sunbird: Forty Poems* (trans. Bruce Berlind *et al.*) Maecenas Press, Budapest, 1997

Gyorgy Faludy, *My Happy Days in Hell* (trans. Kathleen Szasz), Penguin Modern Classics, London, 2010

Gyorgy Faludy, *37 Vers/37 Poems* (trans. Peter Zollman), Maecenas, 2010

Gyorgy Faludy, *Selected Poems* (trans. and ed. Robin Skelton), University of Georgia Press, Athens, 1985

Gyorgy Faludy, *Learn This Poem of Mine by Heart* (ed. John Robert Colombo), Dundurn Books, Toronto, 1983

Gyorgy Faludy, *East and West* (ed. John Robert Colombo) Hounslow Press Toronto, 1978

Mari and George Gomori, (eds.) *I Lived on This Earth*, (trans. George Szirtes *et al.*) Alba, London, 2012

Imre Kertesz, *Fateless*, Vintage, London, 2006

Randolph L. Braham (edited with an introduction by Elie Wiesel) *The Geographical Encyclopaedia of the Holocaust in Hungary,* Northwestern University Press, the US Holocaust Memorial Museum and the Rosenthal Institute for Holocaust Studies at the Graduate Centre, City University of New York, 2013

Randolph L. Braham, *Bibliography of the Holocaust in Hungary*, Columbia University Press and the Rosenthal Institute, 2012

Martin Gilbert, *Churchill and the Jews,* Simon and Schuster, London, 2007

Martin Gilbert, The Holocaust, Holt, Rinehart and Winston, New York, 1985

Desmond Graham (ed.) *Poetry of the Second World War: An International Anthology* Chatto and Windus, London, 1995

Thomas Kabdebo (ed.) *Hundred Hungarian Poems*, Albion Editions, Manchester, 1976

Frigyes Karinthy, *A Journey Round My Skull* (trans. Vernon Duckworth Baker) Corvina, 1992

George Konrad, *A Guest in my Own Country: A Hungarian Life* (trans. Jim Tucker, ed. Michael Henry Heim), The Other Press Books, New York, 2007

George Konrad, *A Feast in the Garden* (Trans. Imre Goldstein), Harcourt, New York, 1992

Paul Lendvai, *Hungary between Democracy and Authoritarianism* (trans. Keith Chester) Hurst, London, 2012

Paul Lendvai, *The Hungarians: A Thousand Years of Victory in Defeat* (trans. Ann Major) Hurst, 2003

Adam Makkai (ed.) *In Quest of the Miracle Stag: an Anthology of Hungarian Poetry from the 13th Century to the Present,* Atlantis- Centaur, Chicago, 2003

Kati Marton, *Enemies of the People: My Family's Journey to America,* Simon and Schuster, New York, 2009

Kati Marton *The Great Escape: Nine Jews who Fled Hitler and Changed the World* Simon and Schuster, 2006

Kati Marton *Wallenberg: Missing Hero,* Random House, 1982

Andras Mezei, *Christmas in Auschwitz* (trans. and ed. Thomas Orszag-Land) Smokestack Books, UK, 2010

Andras Mezei, *Holocaust 1944-2004* (trans. Daniel Danyi, Thomas Orszag-Land and Jon Tarnoc), Belvarosi Press, Budapest, 2004

Andras Mezei, *The Miracle Worker* (trans. Thomas Kabdebo), Belvarosi, 1999

Julie Orringer, *The Invisible Bridge,* Penguin, 2011

Thomas Orszag-Land, *Berlin Proposal*, Envoi Poets Press, Newport, Wales, 1992

Thomas Orszag-Land, *Free Women,* National Poetry Foundation, Fareham, England, 1991

Thomas Orszag-Land, *The Seasons,* Tern Press, Market Drayton, England, 1980

Zsuzsanna Ozsvath,*When the Danube Ran Red,* Syracuse University Press, New York, 2010

Zsuzsanna Ozsvath, *In the Footsteps of Orpheus: The Life and Times of Miklós Radnóti,* Indiana University Press, Bloomington, 2000

Zsuzsanna Ozsvath and Frederick Turner (trans. and ed.) *Light within the Shade: Eight Hundred Years of Hungarian Poetry,* Syracuse, 2014

Alfred Pasternak, *Inhuman Research: Medical Experiments in German Concentration Camps,* Akademiai Press, Budapest, 2006

Patricia and William Oxley (eds.) *Modern Poets of Europe*, Spiny Babbler, Kathmandu, 2003

Katalin Pecsi (ed.), *Salty Coffee: Untold Stories by Jewish Women* (trans. Agnes Merenyi *et al.*) Novella Press, Budapest, 2004

Monica Porter, *Deadly Carousel,* Quartet Books, London, 1990

Miklos Radnoti, *Deathmarch* (trans. Thomas Orszag-Land), The Penniless Press and Snakeskin, both in England, 2009

Miklos Radnoti, *Foaming Sky* (trans. Zsuzsanna Ozsvath and Frederick Turner), Princeton University Press, 1992 and Corvnia, 2002

Hilda Schiff (ed.), *Holocaust Poetry,* Fount Paperbacks, London, 1995

Ernő Szep, *The Smell of Humans: A Memoir of the Holocaust in Hungary*(trans. John Batki), Central European University Press, 1994

Istvan Totfalusi (ed. and trans.) *The Maecenas Anthology of Living Hungarian Poetry,* Maecenas, 1997

Krisztian Ungvary, *Battle for Budapest: 100 Days in World War II* (trans.Ladislus Lob), I. B. Tauris, London, 2003

Miklos Vajda (ed.) *Modern Hungarian Poetry,* Columbia University Press, New York, 1977

THOMAS ORSZÁG-LAND (1938-2018), a Jewish survivor of the Hungarian Holocaust, was a poet and award-winning foreign correspondent

www.ingramcontent.com/pod-product-compliance
Lightning Source LLC
Chambersburg PA
CBHW071021040426
42443CB00007B/887